CHAMELEONS FIND IT PARTICULARLY
DIFFICULT TO DISGUISE THE FACT THAT
THEY'VE BEEN DOWN THE PUB.

THE BESTIE THINGS IN LIFE...

First published in Great Britain in 1998 by
Jarrold Publishing
Whitefriars, Norwich NR3 1TR

BESTIE by Steve Best
Licensed by Paperlink Ltd UK
© Paperlink 1998

ISBN 0-7117-1046-5

All rights reserved. No part of this publication may be reproduced, stored
in a retrieval system or transmitted, in any form or by any means,
electronic, mechanical, photocopying, recording or otherwise,
without the prior permission of the publishers.

Printed in Spain 1/98

THE
BESTIE
THINGS IN LIFE...

Steve Best has been a full-time cartoonist since 1990, contributing regularly to *Punch*, *Private Eye* and other magazines, both in the UK and abroad. His Bestie greetings cards are now among the most successful on the market, reflecting the popularity of his uniquely humorous view of the ridiculous side of life.

MR TORTELLO DENIED THAT HE'D EVER
WORKED FOR THE GODFATHER

THEY INSTINCTIVELY KNEW THE SAFEST PLACE
WHEN HE WAS ABOUT TO PLAY HIS SHOT.

TORTOISE'S LUCK RAN OUT IN THE NEXT EVENT

IT'S BELIEVED THE 'VENUS DE MILO' WAS PROBABLY VANDALISED BY A FEMINIST

ROBINSON'S SPECS WENT DOWN WITH THE SHIP

NOW IT WAS TIME FOR PLAN 'B'

"DON'T EAT THE HARD BIT ON ITS BACK, THEY MAKE YOU FART!"

RODIN'S 'THE LEG-OVER' SUDDENLY
BECAME JUST 'THE KISS.'

"FIRST THINGS FIRST ~ D'YER FANCY SIGNING
FOR LILLIPUT'S BASKETBALL TEAM?"

WHEN VENUS, THE GODDESS OF LOVE, WAS BORN
SHE CHECKED SHE'D GOT EVERYTHING
BEFORE GOING ASHORE

TRANSPORTING BOATLOADS OF CONVICTS TO
AUSTRALIA WASN'T EASY

SAINT FRANCIS OF ASSISI HAD
A VERY CLEVER CAT

THE CATALOGUE HAD PROMISED THAT THE SPECIALLY DESIGNED T-SHIRT WOULD MAKE HIM LOOK LIKE A SEX MACHINE.

DURING HIS MODEL'S LUNCH BREAK
RENOIR GOT HIS ROD OUT.

GOLDILOCKS WAS DELIGHTED TO SEE
ALL THE LITTLE CREATURES WHEN
LOST IN THE FOREST. ~ AT LEAST
SHE KNEW SHE WOULDN'T GO HUNGRY!

"LOOKS LIKE THE VIRTUAL REALITY
COMPUTER'S GONE DOWN ON HIM AGAIN"

AFTER PINOCCHIO TURNED INTO A REAL BOY
GEPPETTO TRIED HIS LUCK AGAIN.

BY ABOUT 2050 B.C. MAN HAD COME VERY CLOSE TO INVENTING THE SWEAR WORD

STUDIES OF DOLPHINS HAVE SHOWN THEY HAVE
THE SAME INTELLECTUAL LEVEL AS
THE AVERAGE MAN

FATHER WAS DOWN THE PUB
COMPLETELY RAT ARSED.

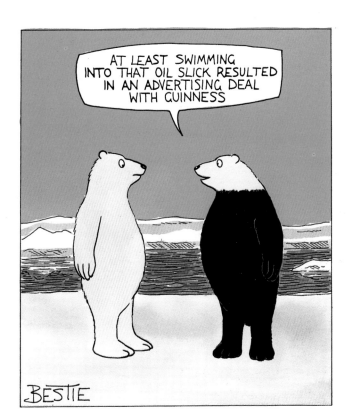

EDISON HAD MANY FAILURES BEFORE HE
PERFECTED THE ELECTRIC LIGHT BULB

A MALE BLACK WIDOW SPIDER DISCOVERS
HIS NEW LOVER IS A VEGETARIAN

ALL THE VILLAGERS BREATHED
A HUGE SIGH OF RELIEF

THE MOTHER SHIP

DAY DREAMING ABOUT YOUR LOVER
CAN BE HAZARDOUS

'SALLY' THE KILLER WHALE,
COULDN'T TAKE ANY MORE HUMILIATION

MONA WAS TRYING NOT TO SMILE AS
SHE WAITED FOR HER SILENT FART
TO REACH LEONARDO.

THE MAKERS OF THE EMPERORS NEW CLOTHES
ALSO SOLD HIM A ROTTWEILER

BRITAIN'S TOP-SECRET REVOLUTIONARY HULL
COULD PROVE DECISIVE IN THE AMERICA'S CUP.

THE U.S. MARINES IN THE PACIFIC WERE
DETERMINED NOT TO MISS THE SUPERBOWL

SUDDENLY TERROR STRUCK
~ HE'D NEVER SEEN A NAKED WOMAN BEFORE

ISADORA WOULD SOON WISH SHE'D WORN
HER SENSIBLE TWO-PIECE

THEY TRIED EVERYTHING TO STOP THE MEN
TALKING ABOUT SPORT.